Introduction

Step inside these pages and embark on an enlightening journey across our planet's breathtaking tapestry. As diverse as Earth's landscapes are its stories, legacies, and wonders that have inspired poets, adventurers, and scholars throughout the ages.

Begin your expedition by scaling the heights of **World Cities**, where every alley and avenue whisper tales of time. Be captivated by the **Famous Landmarks** that stand as testaments to human and natural marvels. Delve deep into the heartbeats of **Cultures and Traditions**, understanding the rituals and rites that define societies. Stand awestruck before **Natural Wonders** that showcase Earth's raw beauty and navigate the vastness of **Oceans & Seas** —our planet's mysterious blue heart.

Feel the rhythm of **Climate & Weather**, which shapes our daily lives, and meander along the serene paths of **Rivers & Lakes**, nature's lifelines. Marvel at the architectural genius behind **Human-Made Wonders** and set sail to the intriguing **Islands of the World**. Let **Flags and Emblems** narrate stories of pride and identity and surrender to the allure of **Urban Legends & Myths**—those whispered tales that straddle truth and imagination.

Breathe in the diversity of **Flora and Fauna**, our planet's myriad lifeforms, and let your senses dance with the delectable delights of **World Cuisine**.

This isn't just a quiz book—it's an invitation. An invitation to explore, to learn, and to celebrate the wonders that bind us together in this beautiful dance of life on Earth. So, ready your compass, sharpen your pencil, and let the journey begin!

Table of Contents

QUESTIONS

World Cities

Easy:

1. Which city is known as "The Big Apple"?
   a) Los Angeles
   b) New York City
   c) Miami
   d) Chicago

2. In which city can you find the Eiffel Tower?
   a) Berlin
   b) Rome
   c) Madrid
   d) Paris

3. Which city is known for its canals and gondolas?
   a) Florence
   b) Venice
   c) Amsterdam
   d) Dublin

4. The Great Wall of China is closest to which major city?
   a) Beijing
   b) Shanghai
   c) Tokyo
   d) Seoul

5. Which city is known as the "City of Love"?
   a) Madrid
   b) Paris
   c) Milan
   d) Brussels

6. Where is the famous Copacabana Beach located?
   a) Rio de Janeiro
   b) Buenos Aires
   c) Havana
   d) Mexico City

7. The Colosseum is a historical landmark in which city?
   a) Athens
   b) Rome
   c) Lisbon
   d) Madrid

8. Which city is home to the Bollywood film industry?
   a) Mumbai
   b) Bangkok
   c) Jakarta
   d) Delhi

9. The Statue of Liberty was a gift from which country?
   a) United Kingdom
   b) Germany
   c) France
   d) Spain

10. In which city is the famous "Red Square" located?
    a) Berlin
    b) Moscow
    c) Beijing
    d) Istanbul

Intermediate:

1. Which city was formerly known as Constantinople?
   a) Athens
   b) Istanbul
   c) Cairo
   d) Rome

2. Which is the southernmost capital city in the world?
   a) Sydney
   b) Buenos Aires
   c) Wellington
   d) Santiago

3. Which city is sometimes called "The Venice of the North"?
   a) Stockholm
   b) Amsterdam
   c) Copenhagen
   d) Dublin

4. In which city is the world's tallest building, the Burj Khalifa, located?
   a) Abu Dhabi
   b) Doha
   c) Dubai
   d) Riyadh

5. Petra, a historical archaeological city, is located in which country?
   a) Greece
   b) Jordan
   c) Turkey
   d) Israel

6. The temple Angkor Wat is located near which city?
   a) Phnom Penh
   b) Hanoi
   c) Siem Reap
   d) Yangon

7. Which city is famous for its carnival and samba dances?
   a) Buenos Aires
   b) Rio de Janeiro
   c) Havana
   d) Montevideo

8. Timbuktu, known for its ancient libraries, is in which country?
   a) Mali
   b) Algeria
   c) Chad
   d) Niger

9. The Rialto Bridge and Doge's Palace are landmarks in which city?
   a) Barcelona
   b) Venice
   c) Prague
   d) Vienna

10. Which city is known for its yearly Running of the Bulls festival?
   a) Seville
   b) Pamplona
   c) Barcelona
   d) Madrid

Challenging:

1. Which city is built on 14 islands connected by over 50 bridges?
   a) Oslo
   b) Stockholm
   c) Helsinki
   d) Reykjavik

2. Which city, also known as "Pearl of the Orient", was once a Portuguese colony?
   a) Goa
   b) Macau
   c) Malacca
   d) Sao Paulo

3. In which city is the historic Umayyad Mosque located?
   a) Cairo
   b) Mecca
   c) Jerusalem
   d) Damascus

4. Which city houses the headquarters of the European Union?
   a) Strasbourg
   b) Geneva
   c) Brussels
   d) Berlin

5. Which city is built on two continents, Europe and Asia?
   a) Istanbul
   b) Moscow
   c) Baku
   d) Athens

6. Arequipa, known as the "White City", is located in which country?
   a) Chile
   b) Bolivia
   c) Peru
   d) Colombia

7. The city of Oporto gave its name to which type of wine?
   a) Champagne
   b) Merlot
   c) Shiraz
   d) Port

8. Which city was historically known as Byzantium before it was renamed Constantinople?
   a) Alexandria
   b) Antioch
   c) Istanbul
   d) Thessaloniki

9. In which city is the Apartheid Museum located?
   a) Cape Town
   b) Nairobi
   c) Johannesburg
   d) Dar es Salaam

10. The world's first underground railway system was opened in which city in 1863?
   a) Paris
   b) London
   c) New York
   d) Tokyo

Expert:

1. Which city is known as the "City of a Thousand Minarets"?
   a) Istanbul
   b) Marrakech
   c) Cairo
   d) Riyadh

2. Which city was historically known as "Eboracum" in ancient times?
   a) York
   b) Rome
   c) Athens
   d) Dublin

3. In which city can you find the ancient rock-hewn churches of Lalibela?
   a) Asmara
   b) Addis Ababa
   c) Lalibela
   d) Khartoum

4. Dushanbe is the capital of which country?
   a) Kazakhstan
   b) Kyrgyzstan
   c) Tajikistan
   d) Turkmenistan

5. Which city is the capital of the island nation of Palau?
   a) Majuro
   b) Honiara
   c) Koror
   d) Nauru

6. The ancient city of Carthage was located near which modern-day capital?
   a) Tripoli
   b) Algiers
   c) Tunis
   d) Rabat

7. Ulaanbaatar is the capital of which country?
   a) Mongolia
   b) Bhutan
   c) Nepal
   d) Myanmar

8. The ancient ruins of Persepolis are located near which modern-day city?
   a) Baghdad
   b) Tehran
   c) Shiraz
   d) Kabul

9. Which city was formerly known as Saigon?
   a) Phnom Penh
   b) Bangkok
   c) Hanoi
   d) Ho Chi Minh City

10. The ancient city of Nineveh was located near which modern-day city?
   a) Aleppo
   b) Mosul
   c) Damascus
   d) Baghdad

Famous Landmarks

Easy:

1. Which country is home to the Eiffel Tower?
   a) Spain
   b) Germany
   c) France
   d) Italy

2. The Great Wall can be found in which country?
   a) China
   b) Japan
   c) Russia
   d) India

3. In which country is the Colosseum located?
   a) Greece
   b) Italy
   c) Turkey
   d) Spain

4. The Statue of Liberty was gifted to the US by which country?
   a) France
   b) Canada
   c) United Kingdom
   d) Spain

5. In which city can you visit the Christ the Redeemer statue?
   a) Buenos Aires
   b) Santiago
   c) Rio de Janeiro
   d) Lima

6. The Taj Mahal is a landmark in which country?
   a) India
   b) Pakistan
   c) Nepal
   d) Bangladesh

7. Stonehenge is located in which country?
   a) Ireland
   b) Scotland
   c) England
   d) Wales

8. In which city can you find the famous Sydney Opera House?
   a) Melbourne
   b) Perth
   c) Brisbane
   d) Sydney

9. Which country is home to the pyramids of Giza?
   a) Iraq
   b) Jordan
   c) Egypt
   d) Saudi Arabia

10. The Leaning Tower is located in which Italian city?
   a) Venice
   b) Pisa
   c) Florence
   d) Rome

Intermediate:

1. Mount Rushmore, which features the faces of four US presidents, is located in which state?
   a) Montana
   b) Wyoming
   c) South Dakota
   d) North Dakota

2. Where can you find the ancient city of Petra?
   a) Iraq
   b) Jordan
   c) Lebanon
   d) Israel

3. The Acropolis is a landmark in which city?
   a) Rome
   b) Athens
   c) Madrid
   d) Lisbon

4. The Burj Khalifa, the tallest building in the world, is in which city?
   a) Doha
   b) Abu Dhabi
   c) Dubai
   d) Riyadh

5. The famous Easter Island statues, known as Moai, belong to which country?
   a) New Zealand
   b) Indonesia
   c) Chile
   d) Fiji

6. In which city is the famous temple of Angkor Wat located?
   a) Phnom Penh
   b) Bangkok
   c) Yangon
   d) Siem Reap

7. The Brandenburg Gate is a landmark in which city?
   a) Vienna
   b) Berlin
   c) Brussels
   d) Amsterdam

8. Neuschwanstein Castle, which inspired Disney's Cinderella Castle, is in which country?
   a) Switzerland
   b) Austria
   c) Germany
   d) France

9. The iconic Golden Gate Bridge is located in which US city?
   a) Los Angeles
   b) New York City
   c) Seattle
   d) San Francisco

10. In which city would you find the Temple of Heaven?
   a) Shanghai
   b) Beijing
   c) Tokyo
   d) Seoul

Challenging:

1. The Atomium, a building shaped like an iron crystal magnified 165 billion times, is in which city?
   a) Brussels
   b) Paris
   c) Vienna
   d) Zurich

2. The Uffizi Gallery, famous for its outstanding collection of Renaissance artworks, is in which city?
   a) Rome
   b) Milan
   c) Venice
   d) Florence

3. The ancient ruins of Machu Picchu are located in which country?
   a) Bolivia
   b) Ecuador
   c) Peru
   d) Colombia

4. The historic Tower of London houses which famous collection of jewels?
   a) The Balmoral Jewels
   b) The Buckingham Jewels
   c) The Royal Crown Jewels
   d) The Windsor Jewels

5. "La Sagrada Família", a large unfinished Roman Catholic church, is in which city?
   a) Madrid
   b) Barcelona
   c) Seville
   d) Valencia

6. Ait Benhaddou, a historic clay city often used in film sets, is located in which country?
   a) Algeria
   b) Tunisia
   c) Morocco
   d) Egypt

7. The famous Mont Saint-Michel, a tidal island and mainland commune, is located in which country?
   a) Italy
   b) Spain
   c) France
   d) Portugal

8. Where would you find the historic volcanic city of Pompeii?
   a) Spain
   b) Greece
   c) Italy
   d) Turkey

9. The Guggenheim Museum, designed by Frank Lloyd Wright, is a prominent attraction in which city?
   a) Chicago
   b) Los Angeles
   c) New York City
   d) Miami

10. The Giant's Causeway, a natural formation of interlocking basalt columns, is located in which part of the UK?
   a) Scotland
   b) Wales
   c) Northern Ireland
   d) England

Expert:

1. Where would you find the Svalbard Global Seed Vault, which is meant to be a backup of seed samples from the world's crops?
   a) Greenland
   b) Finland
   c) Norway
   d) Iceland

2. The Meteora monasteries, built atop natural sandstone rock pillars, are located in which country?
   a) Cyprus
   b) Greece
   c) Bulgaria
   d) Turkey

3. The "Door to Hell", a natural gas field that has been burning since 1971, is found in which country?
   a) Kazakhstan
   b) Uzbekistan
   c) Turkmenistan
   d) Kyrgyzstan

4. Which country is home to the Chand Baori stepwell, one of the deepest and largest stepwells in the world?
   a) India
   b) Nepal
   c) Bangladesh
   d) Pakistan

5. In which city would you find the historic Djinguereber Mosque, constructed in the 14th century?
   a) Cairo
   b) Timbuktu
   c) Addis Ababa
   d) Marrakech

6. The historic Q'eswachaka rope bridge, made of grass and rebuilt annually, spans a gorge in which country?
   a) Chile
   b) Bolivia
   c) Peru
   d) Ecuador

7. The Leshan Giant Buddha, the largest stone Buddha in the world, is located in which country?
   a) Japan
   b) South Korea
   c) China
   d) Vietnam

8. The Ħal Saflieni Hypogeum, a subterranean structure dating to the Saflieni phase (3300-3000 BC), is located in which country?
   a) Malta
   b) Cyprus
   c) Monaco
   d) San Marino

9. The historic city of Palmyra, known for its ruins, is in which modern-day country?
   a) Syria
   b) Jordan
   c) Lebanon
   d) Iraq

10. The ancient archaeological site of Göbekli Tepe, which dates back to the 10th-8th millennium BC, is located in which country?
   a) Iran
   b) Turkey
   c) Israel
   d) Armenia

Cultures and Traditions

Easy:

1. Which country is known for its tradition of afternoon tea?
   a) France
   b) Australia
   c) England
   d) Germany

2. The festival of Diwali is primarily celebrated in which religion?
   a) Christianity
   b) Islam
   c) Hinduism
   d) Buddhism

3. In which country is it traditional to break a plate and shout "Opa!" at celebrations?
   a) Italy
   b) Russia
   c) Greece
   d) Spain

4. Which country celebrates the Day of the Dead in early November?
   a) Mexico
   b) Brazil
   c) Egypt
   d) Japan

5. The traditional Maori war dance is known as the...?
   a) Tango
   b) Samba
   c) Hula
   d) Haka

6. Sushi originates from which country?
   a) China
   b) Korea
   c) Japan
   d) Vietnam

7. Which country is known for the Carnival festival, especially in Rio de Janeiro?
   a) Argentina
   b) Brazil
   c) Colombia
   d) Peru

8. The Eiffel Tower is a popular place for what activity on New Year's Eve?
   a) Fireworks
   b) Kite flying
   c) River diving
   d) Parachuting

9. In which country is it traditional to have a siesta (an afternoon nap)?
   a) Italy
   b) Spain
   c) France
   d) Portugal

10. Bagpipes are a traditional musical instrument of which country?
   a) Ireland
   b) Norway
   c) Scotland
   d) Wales

Intermediate:

1. Which festival involves throwing brightly colored powder at one another?
   a) Songkran
   b) Tomatina
   c) Oktoberfest
   d) Holi

2. The practice of Feng Shui originated in which country?
   a) Japan
   b) China
   c) Vietnam
   d) Thailand

3. Which country is known for its tradition of "Midsummer"?
   a) Sweden
   b) Germany
   c) Australia
   d) Canada

4. Bollywood, a large film industry, is based in which country?
   a) Indonesia
   b) India
   c) Bangladesh
   d) Pakistan

5. Matryoshka dolls, also known as nesting dolls, originate from which country?
   a) Ukraine
   b) Russia
   c) Poland
   d) Belarus

6. The Day of Silence, or Nyepi, is a tradition in which predominantly Hindu island?
   a) Bali
   b) Java
   c) Lombok
   d) Sumatra

7. Which African country is known for its Maasai warriors?
   a) Kenya
   b) Nigeria
   c) Egypt
   d) South Africa

8. Where is the traditional dance known as Flamenco from?
   a) Mexico
   b) Portugal
   c) Spain
   d) Argentina

9. Which country has a tradition of eating KFC for Christmas dinner due to a successful marketing campaign?
   a) South Korea
   b) Japan
   c) China
   d) Philippines

10. In which country would you find the ancient tradition of "Whirling Dervishes"?
   a) India
   b) Iran
   c) Turkey
   d) Saudi Arabia

Challenging:

1. The indigenous Ainu people are native to which country?
   a) New Zealand
   b) Canada
   c) Russia
   d) Japan

2. Which festival in Spain involves running in front of bulls?
   a) San Fermin
   b) La Tomatina
   c) Dia de Reyes
   d) Semana Santa

3. In which country would you attend a traditional "Poi" dance performance?
   a) Fiji
   b) Hawaii
   c) Samoa
   d) Tonga

4. The traditional "Wayang Kulit" shadow puppet theatre comes from...?
   a) Thailand
   b) Indonesia
   c) Cambodia
   d) Malaysia

5. The "Inti Raymi" festival, celebrating the sun god, is a tradition in which country?
   a) Brazil
   b) Ecuador
   c) Peru
   d) Bolivia

6. The "Berber" people are indigenous to which region?
  a) Northern Australia
  b) Central Asia
  c) Northern Africa
  d) Southern Europe

7. In which country would you witness the tradition of eagle hunting?
  a) Mongolia
  b) Kazakhstan
  c) China
  d) Nepal

8. In which country is the tradition of "crying over rice" practiced by brides before their wedding?
  a) India
  b) China
  c) Japan
  d) South Korea

9. The tradition of "Gagaku", an ancient imperial court music and dance, is from which country?
  a) China
  b) Japan
  c) South Korea
  d) Thailand

10. Which Middle Eastern country is known for the traditional dance called "Dabke"?
  a) Jordan
  b) Saudi Arabia
  c) Lebanon
  d) Iran

Expert:

1. In the "Famadihana" tradition, families exhume and re-wrap the remains of their ancestors. Where is this practiced?
   a) Papua New Guinea
   b) Madagascar
   c) Tanzania
   d) Fiji

2. The "Aka" polyphonic singing style, recognized by UNESCO, is from which region?
   a) Central Africa
   b) Siberia
   c) Balkans
   d) Andes

3. The "Lucia" tradition, involving a girl wearing a crown of candles, is celebrated in...?
   a) Iceland
   b) Greenland
   c) Norway
   d) Sweden

4. The "Sami" people, known for their reindeer herding, are native to which region?
   a) Lapland
   b) Siberia
   c) Alps
   d) Patagonia

5. "J'ouvert", a large street party involving paint and mud, marks the beginning of Carnival in which region?
   a) Brazil
   b) Trinidad and Tobago
   c) Spain
   d) Bahamas

6. The "Koryo-saram" are the ethnic Korean minority of which country?
    a) Japan
    b) China
    c) Uzbekistan
    d) North Korea

7. The ancient "Kumari" tradition, involving a living goddess, is practiced in which country?
    a) Nepal
    b) India
    c) Myanmar
    d) Bhutan

8. Which country celebrates the "Wren Day" on December 26, where people dress up and hunt a fake wren?
    a) Ireland
    b) Scotland
    c) Wales
    d) England

9. The "Sardana" is a traditional circle dance of which region?
    a) Basque Country
    b) Galicia
    c) Catalonia
    d) Andalusia

10. The "Ainu" people perform the "Iomante" ritual, which involves the sacrifice of what animal?
    a) Bear
    b) Deer
    c) Eagle
    d) Wolf

Natural Wonders

Easy:

1. Which natural wonder is known as the "Roof of the World"?
   a) Mount Everest
   b) Grand Canyon
   c) Amazon Rainforest
   d) Great Barrier Reef

2. Niagara Falls borders which two countries?
   a) USA and Mexico
   b) USA and Canada
   c) Canada and Greenland
   d) USA and Cuba

3. Which country is home to the Amazon Rainforest?
   a) Brazil
   b) Argentina
   c) Colombia
   d) Peru

4. The Sahara Desert is located on which continent?
   a) Asia
   b) Australia
   c) Africa
   d) North America

5. The Great Barrier Reef is located off the coast of which country?
   a) New Zealand
   b) Australia
   c) Indonesia
   d) Fiji

6. Which US state is home to the Grand Canyon?
   a) California
   b) Nevada
   c) Arizona
   d) Utah

7. Mount Kilimanjaro is located in which country?
   a) Kenya
   b) South Africa
   c) Tanzania
   d) Uganda

8. The Dead Sea is bordered by Jordan and...?
   a) Egypt
   b) Israel
   c) Saudi Arabia
   d) Syria

9. Where can you find the world's largest salt flat, Salar de Uyuni?
   a) Bolivia
   b) Argentina
   c) Chile
   d) Peru

10. Victoria Falls is located on the border of Zambia and...?
   a) Kenya
   b) Zimbabwe
   c) Botswana
   d) Namibia

Intermediate:

1. The Aurora Borealis, also known as the Northern Lights, is most commonly seen in which region?
   a) Equator
   b) Southern Hemisphere
   c) Tropics
   d) Arctic Circle

2. Which country is home to the unique Chocolate Hills?
   a) Philippines
   b) Indonesia
   c) Thailand
   d) Malaysia

3. The Galápagos Islands belong to which country?
   a) Ecuador
   b) Chile
   c) Peru
   d) Colombia

4. Which natural wonder is known for its geothermal activity, including geysers like "Old Faithful"?
   a) Yellowstone National Park
   b) Grand Tetons
   c) Yosemite National Park
   d) Death Valley

5. Ha Long Bay, known for its thousands of limestone islands topped with rainforests, is in which country?
   a) Thailand
   b) Vietnam
   c) Cambodia
   d) Laos

6. Which lake is the deepest in the world?
   a) Lake Superior
   b) Lake Baikal
   c) Lake Tanganyika
   d) Lake Michigan

7. The Giant's Causeway is located in which part of the UK?
   a) Scotland
   b) England
   c) Wales
   d) Northern Ireland

8. Angel Falls, the world's highest uninterrupted waterfall, is located in which country?
   a) Brazil
   b) Argentina
   c) Venezuela
   d) Colombia

9. The Atacama Desert, known as the driest place on Earth, is in...?
   a) Chile
   b) Argentina
   c) Peru
   d) Bolivia

10. The unique rock formations known as "Hoodoos" are prominently found in which national park?
   a) Bryce Canyon National Park
   b) Grand Canyon National Park
   c) Arches National Park
   d) Zion National Park

Challenging:

1. Which island in the Indian Ocean is known for its unique stone formations called the "Giant's Tea Cups"?
   a) Madagascar
   b) Seychelles
   c) Mauritius
   d) Maldives

2. The Door to Hell, a burning natural gas field, is found in which country?
   a) Kazakhstan
   b) Azerbaijan
   c) Uzbekistan
   d) Turkmenistan

3. Which national park in Croatia is known for its cascading lakes and waterfalls?
   a) Krka National Park
   b) Plitvice Lakes National Park
   c) Risnjak National Park
   d) Paklenica National Park

4. The Pink Lake, also known as Lake Hillier, is located in which country?
   a) Canada
   b) New Zealand
   c) Australia
   d) South Africa

5. The world's largest cave, Son Doong Cave, is located in which country?
   a) Laos
   b) Vietnam
   c) Cambodia
   d) Thailand

6. Aysén's Marble Caves are found in which country?
   a) Argentina
   b) Brazil
   c) Chile
   d) Peru

7. Mount Roraima, a flat-topped mountain that inspired the movie "Up", borders Brazil, Venezuela, and...?
   a) Colombia
   b) Guyana
   c) Suriname
   d) Bolivia

8. The Silfra Fissure, a popular diving site, is the meeting point of two continental plates in which country?
   a) Iceland
   b) Norway
   c) Sweden
   d) Denmark

9. The Okavango Delta, a vast inland river delta, is found in which country?
   a) Botswana
   b) Zambia
   c) Namibia
   d) Angola

10. Mount Thor on Baffin Island has the world's greatest purely vertical drop. In which country is it located?
   a) Canada
   b) Greenland
   c) Russia
   d) Norway

Expert:

1. Which underwater mountain range is the world's longest?
   a) Mid-Atlantic Ridge
   b) Andes
   c) Rocky Mountains
   d) Himalayas

2. The Richat Structure, also known as the "Eye of the Sahara", is located in which country?
   a) Mali
   b) Niger
   c) Mauritania
   d) Chad

3. Which country has the most number of geysers in the world?
   a) USA
   b) New Zealand
   c) Russia
   d) Iceland

4. The "Lost World" tepui, a table-top mountain that inspired Sir Arthur Conan Doyle's novel, is located in which country?
   a) Brazil
   b) Guyana
   c) Venezuela
   d) Colombia

5. Mount Erebus, one of the few consistently active volcanoes, is located on which continent?
   a) Africa
   b) Asia
   c) South America
   d) Antarctica

6. The Danakil Depression, one of the hottest and most inhospitable places on Earth, is located in...?
   a) Eritrea
   b) Djibouti
   c) Ethiopia
   d) Somalia

7. The world's second largest boiling lake is found on which Caribbean island?
   a) Barbados
   b) Jamaica
   c) Dominica
   d) Saint Lucia

8. Socotra Island, known for its alien-like Dragon's Blood trees, is a part of which country?
   a) Yemen
   b) Oman
   c) Saudi Arabia
   d) UAE

9. The Pamukkale, meaning "cotton castle" in Turkish, known for its terraces of carbonate minerals, is located in...?
   a) Greece
   b) Turkey
   c) Iran
   d) Azerbaijan

10. The Tsingy de Bemaraha National Park, known for its limestone formations, is located in which country?
   a) Madagascar
   b) Comoros
   c) Seychelles
   d) Mauritius

Oceans & Seas

Easy:

1. Which is the largest ocean in the world?
   a) Atlantic Ocean
   b) Indian Ocean
   c) Arctic Ocean
   d) Pacific Ocean

2. Which sea is known for its high salt content making it easy to float?
   a) Dead Sea
   b) Red Sea
   c) Mediterranean Sea
   d) Baltic Sea

3. Which ocean is the smallest?
   a) Atlantic Ocean
   b) Indian Ocean
   c) Arctic Ocean
   d) Pacific Ocean

4. The Titanic sank in which ocean?
   a) Atlantic Ocean
   b) Indian Ocean
   c) Southern Ocean
   d) Pacific Ocean

5. Which sea is the world's largest body of fresh water by volume?
   a) Caribbean Sea
   b) Caspian Sea
   c) Black Sea
   d) Adriatic Sea

6. Which ocean is located at the southernmost part of the world?
   a) Atlantic Ocean
   b) Indian Ocean
   c) Pacific Ocean
   d) Southern Ocean

7. The Bermuda Triangle is located in which ocean?
   a) Atlantic Ocean
   b) Indian Ocean
   c) Pacific Ocean
   d) Arctic Ocean

8. Which of the following is NOT an ocean?
   a) Caribbean
   b) Arctic
   c) Atlantic
   d) Indian

9. The Great Barrier Reef is located in which sea/ocean?
   a) Coral Sea
   b) Tasman Sea
   c) Indian Ocean
   d) Pacific Ocean

10. Which sea is connected to the Atlantic Ocean via the Strait of Gibraltar?
   a) Dead Sea
   b) Adriatic Sea
   c) Mediterranean Sea
   d) Red Sea

Intermediate:

1. The Mariana Trench, the deepest oceanic trench, is located in which ocean?
   a) Atlantic Ocean
   b) Pacific Ocean
   c) Indian Ocean
   d) Southern Ocean

2. Which of these seas is the world's largest inland body of water by area?
   a) North Sea
   b) Black Sea
   c) Caspian Sea
   d) Aegean Sea

3. The Sargasso Sea is unique because it is surrounded by...?
   a) Land
   b) Icebergs
   c) Ocean currents
   d) Coral reefs

4. Which ocean surrounds the Maldives?
   a) Atlantic Ocean
   b) Arctic Ocean
   c) Indian Ocean
   d) Pacific Ocean

5. Which sea separates Italy from the Balkan Peninsula?
   a) Tyrrhenian Sea
   b) Ionian Sea
   c) Adriatic Sea
   d) Ligurian Sea

6. The Sea of Japan is bordered by Japan and...?
   a) China
   b) Russia
   c) Philippines
   d) South Korea

7. Which ocean is the third largest, covering about 20% of the Earth's water surface?
   a) Atlantic Ocean
   b) Arctic Ocean
   c) Indian Ocean
   d) Pacific Ocean

8. The Bay of Bengal is the northeastern part of which ocean?
   a) Atlantic Ocean
   b) Pacific Ocean
   c) Indian Ocean
   d) Southern Ocean

9. The Gulf Stream, a major ocean current, originates in which ocean?
   a) Pacific Ocean
   b) Indian Ocean
   c) Atlantic Ocean
   d) Arctic Ocean

10. The Arafura Sea is located between Australia and which country?
   a) New Zealand
   b) Papua New Guinea
   c) Indonesia
   d) Fiji

Challenging:

1. Which is the shallowest ocean in the world?
   a) Atlantic Ocean
   b) Pacific Ocean
   c) Indian Ocean
   d) Arctic Ocean

2. The Laptev Sea is part of which ocean?
   a) Atlantic Ocean
   b) Pacific Ocean
   c) Arctic Ocean
   d) Indian Ocean

3. The Andaman Sea is located off the coast of which country?
   a) India
   b) Thailand
   c) Philippines
   d) Malaysia

4. Which strait connects the Mediterranean Sea to the Atlantic Ocean?
   a) Strait of Gibraltar
   b) Bosporus Strait
   c) Strait of Hormuz
   d) Panama Strait

5. The Drake Passage lies between which two land masses?
   a) Africa and Europe
   b) Asia and Africa
   c) South America and Antarctica
   d) North America and Asia

6. The Laccadive Sea is off the southwestern coast of which country?
   a) India
   b) Indonesia
   c) Malaysia
   d) Sri Lanka

7. Which gulf lies between Saudi Arabia and Iran?
   a) Gulf of Aden
   b) Gulf of Oman
   c) Persian Gulf
   d) Gulf of Suez

8. The Barents Sea is located north of which country?
   a) Canada
   b) Norway
   c) Russia
   d) Greenland

9. Which of these seas has no coastline and is entirely surrounded by ocean currents?
   a) Celebes Sea
   b) Sargasso Sea
   c) Beaufort Sea
   d) East Siberian Sea

10. The Bellingshausen Sea is part of which ocean?
    a) Atlantic Ocean
    b) Arctic Ocean
    c) Indian Ocean
    d) Southern Ocean

Expert:

1. Which Sea is the northernmost arm of the Mediterranean Sea?
   a) Aegean Sea
   b) Adriatic Sea
   c) Ionian Sea
   d) Ligurian Sea

2. Which Sea is bounded by Kazakhstan to the northeast and Iran to the south?
   a) Caspian Sea
   b) Black Sea
   c) North Sea
   d) Aegean Sea

3. The Coral Triangle, known for its marine biodiversity, does NOT include which of the following countries?
   a) Indonesia
   b) Malaysia
   c) Philippines
   d) India

4. Which Ocean has the world's largest area of oceanic dead zones?
   a) Pacific Ocean
   b) Atlantic Ocean
   c) Indian Ocean
   d) Arctic Ocean

5. Which strait is located between Greenland and Iceland?
   a) Davis Strait
   b) Denmark Strait
   c) Fram Strait
   d) Bering Strait

6. Which of the following is NOT a marginal sea of the Arctic Ocean?
   a) Chukchi Sea
   b) Beaufort Sea
   c) Tasman Sea
   d) Laptev Sea

7. The Weddell Sea is situated off the coast of which continent?
   a) Africa
   b) South America
   c) Antarctica
   d) Australia

8. Which gulf is located to the west of the Florida peninsula?
   a) Gulf of California
   b) Gulf of Mexico
   c) Gulf of Aden
   d) Gulf of Guinea

9. The Salish Sea includes parts of which two countries?
   a) USA and Canada
   b) Norway and Sweden
   c) Australia and New Zealand
   d) Russia and China

10. The Scotia Sea is located near which tectonic plate boundary?
   a) Divergent boundary
   b) Convergent boundary
   c) Transform boundary
   d) Plateau boundary

Climate & Weather

Easy:

1. What does a thermometer measure?
   a) Pressure
   b) Humidity
   c) Temperature
   d) Wind speed

2. Which of the following is NOT a type of precipitation?
   a) Snow
   b) Hail
   c) Dew
   d) Rain

3. What is the main gas responsible for the greenhouse effect?
   a) Oxygen
   b) Nitrogen
   c) Hydrogen
   d) Carbon dioxide

4. Which of the following climates is typically the driest?
   a) Desert
   b) Tropical rainforest
   c) Tundra
   d) Savanna

5. What is a tornado?
   a) A snowstorm
   b) A dust storms
   c) A rotating column of air
   d) A heavy rainfall

6. In which layer of the atmosphere does weather occur?
   a) Troposphere
   b) Mesosphere
   c) Thermosphere
   d) Stratosphere

7. What do you call the boundary between two different air masses?
   a) Isobar
   b) Front
   c) Isotherm
   d) Cyclone

8. Which of the following is NOT a type of cloud?
   a) Cirrus
   b) Cumulus
   c) Nebulus
   d) Stratus

9. What type of weather does a red sky at morning usually predict?
   a) Clear skies
   b) Rain or stormy weather
   c) Snow
   d) No change

10. What is the name of the scale used to measure the strength of tornadoes?
    a) Mercalli scale
    b) Richter scale
    c) Beaufort scale
    d) Fujita scale

Intermediate:

1. Which of these is a characteristic of the Mediterranean climate?
   a) Frequent tornadoes
   b) Hot and humid summers
   c) Mild and wet summers
   d) Warm and dry summers

2. What phenomenon causes the periodic warming of the Pacific Ocean?
   a) Gulf Stream
   b) El Niño
   c) Atlantic Multidecadal Oscillation
   d) North Atlantic Drift

3. What's the main difference between weather and climate?
   a) They mean the same thing.
   b) Weather is short-term, climate is long-term.
   c) Climate is short-term, weather is long-term.
   d) Weather measures temperature, climate measures pressure.

4. Which of the following areas will most likely experience a monsoon?
   a) Sahara Desert
   b) Southwestern U.S.
   c) Central Africa
   d) South Asia

5. What is the driest place on Earth?
   a) Sahara Desert
   b) Kalahari Desert
   c) Gobi Desert
   d) Atacama Desert

6. Which gas is the most abundant in the Earth's atmosphere?
   a) Oxygen
   b) Carbon dioxide
   c) Argon
   d) Nitrogen

7. What type of cloud is often associated with thunderstorms?
   a) Cumulus
   b) Stratus
   c) Cirrus
   d) Cumulonimbus

8. Which Ocean is most affected by the phenomenon known as "The Blob" of unusually warm water?
   a) Atlantic
   b) Indian
   c) Pacific
   d) Arctic

9. Which of the following cities is known for its "mistral" wind?
   a) Paris, France
   b) London, U.K.
   c) Mumbai, India
   d) Marseille, France

10. What is a haboob?
   a) A rainstorm
   b) An intense dust storms
   c) A type of tornado
   d) A cold front

Challenging:

1. What climate phenomenon is responsible for a collapse in anchovy fisheries off the coast of South America?
   a) El Niño
   b) The Blob
   c) North Atlantic Drift
   d) Indian Ocean Dipole

2. Which city is known as the world's "wettest place"?
   a) Mawsynram, India
   b) Cherrapunji, India
   c) Manaus, Brazil
   d) Kuala Lumpur, Malaysia

3. What is the name of the high-altitude wind that moves from west to east?
   a) Trade wind
   b) Polar easterlies
   c) Jet stream
   d) Prevailing westerlies

4. The Köppen climate classification system denotes "Dfc" as which kind of climate?
   a) Tropical rainforest
   b) Desert
   c) Subarctic
   d) Mediterranean

5. Which layer of the atmosphere lies immediately above the stratosphere?
   a) Troposphere
   b) Mesosphere
   c) Exosphere
   d) Thermosphere

6. What term describes the shifting of wind directions with height, often leading to tornadic activity?
   a) Wind shear
   b) Wind gradient
   c) Updraft
   d) Vortex

7. Which phenomenon results in decreased rainfall over Indonesia and Australia?
   a) El Niño
   b) La Niña
   c) Gulf Stream
   d) The Blob

8. Which desert experiences the phenomenon of "singing sands" or "booming dunes"?
   a) Sahara Desert
   b) Gobi Desert
   c) Sonoran Desert
   d) Kalahari Desert

9. What does a barometer measure?
   a) Temperature
   b) Atmospheric pressure
   c) Humidity
   d) Wind speed

10. Which area is often referred to as the "Roof of the World" due to its high altitude and harsh climate?
   a) Andes Mountains
   b) Himalayas
   c) Alps
   d) Rocky Mountains

Expert:

1. What is virga?
   a) Rain that evaporates before reaching the ground
   b) A type of supercell thunderstorm
   c) The highest cloud formation
   d) A rare type of snowfall

2. The ITCZ (Intertropical Convergence Zone) is known for what?
   a) Cold fronts and polar air
   b) Dry, desert conditions
   c) Heavy precipitation and thunderstorms
   d) Consistent wind patterns suitable for sailing

3. Which climate type would you most likely find at high elevations in the tropics?
   a) Desert
   b) Tundra
   c) Alpine
   d) Oceanic

4. What is the primary driver of the ocean's thermohaline circulation?
   a) Wind patterns
   b) Differences in salinity and temperature
   c) Tectonic plate movement
   d) The Coriolis effect

5. Polar vortexes are most commonly associated with which layer of the atmosphere?
   a) Troposphere
   b) Stratosphere
   c) Mesosphere
   d) Thermosphere

6. In what part of the world would you find the "Föhn" wind?
    a) Southwestern United States
    b) Central Asia
    c) The Alps in Europe
    d) Australian outback

7. Which of these events can result in a sudden and significant temperature drop, referred to as a "cold drop"?
    a) Cyclones
    b) Anticyclones
    c) DANA (Depresión Aislada en Niveles Altos)
    d) Jet streams

8. What phenomenon causes "blood rain," where rain has a reddish appearance due to desert dust?
    a) Sahara Air Layer
    b) Australian Dust Bowl
    c) El Niño
    d) Arctic blast

9. Which of these is a significant consequence of the urban heat island effect?
    a) Increased snowfall in cities
    b) Cities having cooler nights than rural areas
    c) Increase in city temperatures, especially at night
    d) Higher humidity levels in cities

10. What is a microburst?
    a) A miniature tornado
    b) A brief, intense downburst of wind from a thunderstorm
    c) A small rain shower
    d) A short-lived rainbow

Rivers & Lakes

Easy:

1. Which River is the longest in the world?
   a) Amazon
   b) Mississippi
   c) Nile
   d) Yangtze

2. What is the largest lake by surface area?
   a) Lake Superior
   b) Caspian Sea
   c) Lake Victoria
   d) Lake Baikal

3. Where is the River Thames located?
   a) New York
   b) Paris
   c) London
   d) Berlin

4. The Ganges River is sacred to which religion?
   a) Christianity
   b) Buddhism
   c) Hinduism
   d) Islam

5. Which of the following is the deepest lake in the world?
   a) Lake Tanganyika
   b) Lake Baikal
   c) Great Slave Lake
   d) Lake Michigan

6. Into which body of water does the River Nile empty?
   a) Atlantic Ocean
   b) Mediterranean Sea
   c) Red Sea
   d) Dead Sea

7. The Mississippi River flows through which country?
   a) Canada
   b) USA
   c) Brazil
   d) Russia

8. Which of these rivers is the longest in Europe?
   a) Loire
   b) Rhine
   c) Thames
   d) Volga

9. Lake Titicaca is located on the border of Peru and which other country?
   a) Brazil
   b) Bolivia
   c) Argentina
   d) Chile

10. Which of the following lakes is the highest navigable body of water in the world?
   a) Dead Sea
   b) Lake Baikal
   c) Lake Titicaca
   d) Lake Tahoe

Intermediate:

1. Which River flows through the Grand Canyon?
   a) Colorado River
   b) Missouri River
   c) Ohio River
   d) Snake River

2. The Danube River flows through how many countries?
   a) 4
   b) 6
   c) 10
   d) 14

3. Which Lake is known as the "Jewel of the Italian Lakes"?
   a) Lake Garda
   b) Lake Maggiore
   c) Lake Como
   d) Lake Bracciano

4. The Tigris and Euphrates rivers are most closely associated with the history of which ancient civilization?
   a) Mayans
   b) Egyptians
   c) Mesopotamians
   d) Indus Valley

5. Which River is often cited as the geographical divider between Europe and Asia?
   a) Danube
   b) Dnieper
   c) Ural
   d) Don

6. The source of the Amazon River is located in which country?
   a) Brazil
   b) Peru
   c) Colombia
   d) Venezuela

7. Lake Malawi is located in the Great Rift Valley of Africa. Which of the following countries does NOT border it?
   a) Tanzania
   b) Mozambique
   c) Zambia
   d) Uganda

8. Which of the following rivers is NOT one of the five rivers of the Punjab region in India and Pakistan?
   a) Indus
   b) Sutlej
   c) Brahmaputra
   d) Jhelum

9. Lake Geneva is shared by Switzerland and which other country?
   a) Germany
   b) France
   c) Austria
   d) Italy

10. What is the primary outflow of the Great Lakes in North America?
    a) Mississippi River
    b) Colorado River
    c) Saint Lawrence River
    d) Hudson River

Challenging:

1. Which River forms a significant portion of the U.S.-Mexico border?
   a) San Joaquin
   b) Colorado
   c) Brazos
   d) Rio Grande

2. The Mekong River doesn't flow through which of the following countries?
   a) Thailand
   b) Cambodia
   c) Vietnam
   d) Philippines

3. Which Lake is located on the border between Israel, Jordan, and the West Bank?
   a) Dead Sea
   b) Sea of Galilee
   c) Lake Tiberias
   d) Both b) and c)

4. Which River is known as "China's Sorrow" due to its devastating floods?
   a) Yangtze
   b) Yellow River (Huang He)
   c) Pearl River
   d) Mekong River

5. Lake Baikal holds what distinction in terms of volume?
   a) Shallowest lake by volume
   b) Most saline lake by volume
   c) Contains more water than the North American Great Lakes combined
   d) Lowest volume of freshwater for its size

6. Which African river is known for its dramatic waterfalls, including Victoria Falls?
   a) Congo River
   b) Nile River
   c) Orange River
   d) Zambezi River

7. What is the world's largest river by discharge?
   a) Amazon
   b) Congo
   c) Yangtze
   d) Nile

8. Which of the following is NOT a Salt Lake?
   a) Great Salt Lake
   b) Caspian Sea
   c) Aral Sea
   d) Lake Tahoe

9. The Brahmaputra River flows through which of the following mountain ranges?
   a) Andes
   b) Rockies
   c) Himalayas
   d) Ural

10. Which River flows northward into the Mediterranean Sea?
   a) Niger
   b) Congo
   c) Nile
   d) Tigris

Expert:

1. Which River is associated with the Sundarbans mangrove forest?
   a) Brahmaputra
   b) Ganges
   c) Both a) and b)
   d) Yamuna

2. Lake Vostok, a subglacial lake, is located on which continent?
   a) Africa
   b) Asia
   c) Antarctica
   d) North America

3. Which River has the second-largest drainage basin in the world, after the Amazon?
   a) Congo
   b) Yangtze
   c) Mississippi
   d) Nile

4. The Okavango River empties into which unusual destination?
   a) A desert
   b) A mountain range
   c) Another river
   d) A delta

5. Lake Chad is unique because:
   a) It's the deepest lake in the world.
   b) It's the largest freshwater lake by volume.
   c) Its size varies dramatically between wet and dry seasons.
   d) It's completely surrounded by mountains.

6. The Paraná River is located in South America. It merges with another river to form the estuary known as the:
   a) Bay of Pigs
   b) Río de la Plata
   c) Gulf of Darién
   d) Pantanal

7. The Sutlej River plays a significant role in the geography of which country?
   a) China
   b) India
   c) Russia
   d) Egypt

8. Which of the following rivers flows entirely within the Arctic Circle?
   a) Yukon
   b) Lena
   c) Ob
   d) Volga

9. Lake Maracaibo in Venezuela is especially known for:
   a) Its intense blue color.
   b) Its constantly frozen surface.
   c) Its nightly lightning phenomena.
   d) Its underground connection to the sea.

10. The Salween River flows through which of the following countries?
   a) Vietnam and Cambodia
   b) India and Nepal
   c) Myanmar and Thailand
   d) Malaysia and Indonesia

Human-Made Wonders

Easy:

1. Which ancient wonder was found in the city of Babylon?
   a) Hanging Gardens
   b) Statue of Zeus
   c) Colossus of Rhodes
   d) Lighthouse of Alexandria

2. Where can you find the modern wonder known as Christ the Redeemer statue?
   a) Buenos Aires
   b) Rio de Janeiro
   c) Bogota
   d) Santiago

3. The Eiffel Tower is located in which city?
   a) Berlin
   b) Brussels
   c) Paris
   d) Rome

4. Which wonder was located on the island of Rhodes?
   a) Statue of Zeus
   b) Mausoleum at Halicarnassus
   c) Colossus of Rhodes
   d) Temple of Artemis

5. The Great Wall of China was primarily built to protect against invasions from...?
   a) Sea Pirates
   b) Nomadic Tribes
   c) Mountain Tribes
   d) Internal Revolts

6. Which of the following is a large amphitheater in the center of Rome, Italy?
   a) The Parthenon
   b) Notre Dame
   c) Colosseum
   d) Sagrada Família

7. The Taj Mahal is located in which city?
   a) Delhi
   b) Mumbai
   c) Agra
   d) Jaipur

8. Which wonder served as a tomb for Mausolus?
   a) Mausoleum at Halicarnassus
   b) Temple of Artemis
   c) Pyramid of Giza
   d) Hanging Gardens

9. The Sydney Opera House is located in which country?
   a) New Zealand
   b) Canada
   c) Australia
   d) USA

10. Which ancient wonder stood in Olympia?
   a) Hanging Gardens
   b) Statue of Zeus
   c) Lighthouse of Alexandria
   d) Temple of Artemis

Intermediate:

1. Which of the following wonders was rebuilt several times due to earthquakes and other causes?
   a) Temple of Artemis
   b) Colossus of Rhodes
   c) Mausoleum at Halicarnassus
   d) Pyramid of Giza

2. The Burj Khalifa, the tallest building in the world as of the last update, is located in which city?
   a) Riyadh
   b) Doha
   c) Abu Dhabi
   d) Dubai

3. Which human-made wonder connects the Mediterranean Sea to the Red Sea?
   a) Panama Canal
   b) Suez Canal
   c) Grand Canal
   d) Erie Canal

4. The Palace of Versailles is located in which country?
   a) Germany
   b) France
   c) England
   d) Italy

5. Mount Rushmore, with the faces of four U.S. presidents, is located in which state?
   a) Wyoming
   b) Montana
   c) North Dakota
   d) South Dakota

6. The Channel Tunnel connects the UK with which country?
   a) Belgium
   b) Ireland
   c) France
   d) Netherlands

7. Which ancient city, now in ruins, is famous for its intricate stone constructions without the use of mortar?
   a) Chichen Itza
   b) Machu Picchu
   c) Stonehenge
   d) Petra

8. Neuschwanstein Castle, which inspired the design of Disneyland's Sleeping Beauty Castle, is located in which country?
   a) Austria
   b) Switzerland
   c) Germany
   d) France

9. The Golden Gate Bridge is a famous landmark of which city?
   a) Los Angeles
   b) San Diego
   c) New York
   d) San Francisco

10. The Rialto Bridge is a famous landmark in which city?
   a) Venice
   b) Rome
   c) Madrid
   d) Lisbon

Challenging:

1. Which of the following wonders is a prehistoric monument in Wiltshire, England?
   a) Machu Picchu
   b) Colosseum
   c) Stonehenge
   d) Great Wall of China

2. Petra, also known as the 'Rose City' due to the color of the stone from which it is carved, is located in which country?
   a) Egypt
   b) Jordan
   c) Israel
   d) Saudi Arabia

3. The Hagia Sophia, originally a cathedral then a mosque and now a museum, is located in...?
   a) Athens
   b) Istanbul
   c) Rome
   d) Cairo

4. Which of these structures was mainly built during the Ming dynasty?
   a) Forbidden City
   b) Terracotta Army
   c) Great Wall of China
   d) Potala Palace

5. The "Lost City of the Incas" is another name for...?
   a) Tikal
   b) Machu Picchu
   c) Teotihuacan
   d) Angkor Wat

6. The Leaning Tower of Pisa was originally built as a...?
   a) Watch Tower
   b) Lighthouse
   c) Bell Tower
   d) Military Fort

7. Which structure was commissioned by the Mughal Emperor Shah Jahan in memory of his wife Mumtaz Mahal?
   a) Red Fort
   b) Agra Fort
   c) Charminar
   d) Taj Mahal

8. Which of these is the largest brick-built structure in the world?
   a) The Great Wall of China
   b) The Great Pyramid of Giza
   c) The Colosseum
   d) Malbork Castle

9. Where can you find the historic fort known as the Alhambra?
   a) Barcelona, Spain
   b) Granada, Spain
   c) Lisbon, Portugal
   d) Naples, Italy

10. The Kiyomizu-dera, a historic temple, is located in which country?
    a) China
    b) South Korea
    c) Japan
    d) Thailand

Expert:

1. Which of the following wonders is an astronomical clock in Prague?
    a) The Torre dell'Orologio
    b) The Gros Horloge
    c) The Zytglogge
    d) The Prague Orloj

2. Borobudur, the world's largest Buddhist temple, is located in which country?
    a) Myanmar
    b) Cambodia
    c) Thailand
    d) Indonesia

3. Which structure was designed by the Catalan architect Antoni Gaudí and remains incomplete to this day?
    a) The Eiffel Tower
    b) Sagrada Família
    c) Notre Dame Cathedral
    d) The Colosseum

4. Château Frontenac, considered one of the most photographed hotels in the world, is located in which city?
    a) Toronto
    b) Montreal
    c) Vancouver
    d) Quebec City

5. The "Gate of the Sun" is a megalithic solid stone arch or gateway located in which ancient city?
    a) Teotihuacan
    b) Chichen Itza
    c) Tiahuanaco
    d) Angkor Wat

6. The Tsar Bell, the largest bell in the world, can be found in...?
   a) The Kremlin, Moscow
   b) Notre Dame, Paris
   c) Big Ben, London
   d) La Sagrada Família, Barcelona

7. A series of fortifications made of stone, brick, tamped earth, wood, and other materials, primarily built along the northern borders of China is known as?
   a) Hadrian's Wall
   b) Berlin Wall
   c) Great Wall of China
   d) Walls of Constantinople

8. Which of the following is a mausoleum situated in the city of Samarkand, Uzbekistan and is one of the most esteemed sights of Central Asian architecture?
   a) The Gur-e Amir
   b) The Shah-i-Zinda
   c) The Registan
   d) The Bibi-Khanym Mosque

9. The Basilica Cistern, an underground wonder, can be found in which city?
   a) Rome
   b) Athens
   c) Istanbul
   d) Cairo

10. Which wonder is a set of 887 extant monumental statues, called moai, created by the Rapa Nui people on Easter Island?
   a) Nazca Lines
   b) Teotihuacan Pyramids
   c) Easter Island Statues
   d) Stonehenge

Islands of the World

Easy:

1. Which island is known for its Moai statues?
   a) Hawaii
   b) Fiji
   c) Easter Island
   d) Bermuda

2. Where is the island of Bali located?
   a) Philippines
   b) Thailand
   c) Malaysia
   d) Indonesia

3. Which island is known as "The Emerald Isle"?
   a) Iceland
   b) Greenland
   c) Ireland
   d) Sardinia

4. Manhattan is an island that's part of which city?
   a) Chicago
   b) San Francisco
   c) New York City
   d) Boston

5. Which island is famous for its rum?
   a) Jamaica
   b) Bermuda
   c) Cuba
   d) Maldives

6. Which island country is known for its Maori culture?
   a) Australia
   b) Fiji
   c) New Zealand
   d) Samoa

7. Where is the island of Sicily located?
   a) Spain
   b) France
   c) Italy
   d) Greece

8. Which of these islands is the largest in the world?
   a) New Zealand
   b) Madagascar
   c) Borneo
   d) Greenland

9. Which island is famous for its reggae music?
   a) Bahamas
   b) Jamaica
   c) Puerto Rico
   d) Barbados

10. Which island is known for its unique species studied by Charles Darwin?
   a) Galápagos Islands
   b) Falkland Islands
   c) Faroe Islands
   d) Balearic Islands

Intermediate:

1. The Maldives is an archipelago in which ocean?
   a) Atlantic
   b) Indian
   c) Pacific
   d) Arctic

2. Which island is home to the city of Reykjavik?
   a) Faroe Islands
   b) Greenland
   c) Shetland Islands
   d) Iceland

3. Which island is divided between France and Spain?
   a) Ibiza
   b) Majorca
   c) Corsica
   d) Borneo

4. Which island, also a country, is located near the southern tip of India?
   a) Sri Lanka
   b) Maldives
   c) Seychelles
   d) Mauritius

5. Where are the Andaman and Nicobar Islands located?
   a) Caribbean Sea
   b) Mediterranean Sea
   c) Bay of Bengal
   d) South China Sea

6. Which island is associated with the mythical story of the Minotaur?
   a) Rhodes
   b) Santorini
   c) Crete
   d) Cyprus

7. Which is the largest island in the Mediterranean Sea?
   a) Sicily
   b) Sardinia
   c) Malta
   d) Cyprus

8. The island of Sumatra is part of which country?
   a) Malaysia
   b) Indonesia
   c) Philippines
   d) Thailand

9. Where is the Isle of Man located?
   a) Between England and Ireland
   b) Between Scotland and Norway
   c) Between France and England
   d) Between Ireland and Scotland

10. Bora Bora is an island located in which group?
   a) Maldives
   b) Society Islands
   c) Hawaiian Islands
   d) Canary Islands

Challenging:

1. Which island is the largest sand island in the world?
   a) Ellesmere Island
   b) Fraser Island
   c) Java
   d) Luzon

2. The island of Java is part of which country?
   a) Malaysia
   b) Indonesia
   c) Thailand
   d) Philippines

3. Which island is known as "The Island of the Gods"?
   a) Bali
   b) Fiji
   c) Tahiti
   d) Samoa

4. The Komodo dragon is native to which Indonesian island?
   a) Bali
   b) Java
   c) Borneo
   d) Komodo

5. Which island in Canada is known as the "Rock"?
   a) Vancouver Island
   b) Prince Edward Island
   c) Newfoundland
   d) Baffin Island

6. The Seychelles archipelago is located in which ocean?
   a) Atlantic
   b) Indian
   c) Pacific
   d) Arctic

7. Which island is home to the world's smallest capital city (by population), Adamstown?
   a) Pitcairn Island
   b) Nauru
   c) Tuvalu
   d) San Marino

8. Which island group includes Ibiza, Mallorca, and Menorca?
   a) Azores
   b) Canary Islands
   c) Cape Verde
   d) Balearic Islands

9. Which island is known as "The Pearl of the Indian Ocean"?
   a) Mauritius
   b) Maldives
   c) Sri Lanka
   d) Seychelles

10. The ancient city of Knossos is located on which Greek island?
   a) Rhodes
   b) Crete
   c) Santorini
   d) Mykonos

Expert:

1. Which island was formerly known as Formosa?
    a) Taiwan
    b) Hong Kong
    c) Macau
    d) Hainan

2. Which island in the Pacific is known for its mysterious statues called "Moai"?
    a) Fiji
    b) Easter Island
    c) Samoa
    d) Tonga

3. Which is the third largest island in the world after Greenland and New Guinea?
    a) Borneo
    b) Madagascar
    c) Sumatra
    d) Iceland

4. Which island was the site of a historic volcanic eruption in 1883?
    a) Krakatoa
    b) Vesuvius
    c) St. Helens
    d) Etna

5. Which island is known for its "Ring of Fire", a circle of volcanoes?
    a) Sumatra
    b) Hawaii
    c) Java
    d) Luzon

6. On which island would you find the U.S. state of Oahu?
   a) Samoa
   b) Hawaii
   c) Guam
   d) Puerto Rico

7. Which island in the Indian Ocean is known as the "eighth continent" due to its unique biodiversity?
   a) Sri Lanka
   b) Seychelles
   c) Comoros
   d) Madagascar

8. Svalbard is an archipelago located in which ocean?
   a) Arctic Ocean
   b) Atlantic Ocean
   c) Pacific Ocean
   d) Indian Ocean

9. Which island has a native marsupial known as the Tasmanian devil?
   a) New Zealand
   b) Fiji
   c) Tasmania
   d) Guam

10. The Arenal Volcano is located on which Central American island?
   a) Isla de Ometepe
   b) Roatán
   c) Cozumel
   d) None of the above (it's in Costa Rica, which is not an island)

Flags and Emblems

Easy:

1. Which country's flag has a maple leaf in the center?
   a) New Zealand
   b) Australia
   c) Canada
   d) Norway

2. Which of these flags consists of only red and white stripes?
   a) USA
   b) Germany
   c) Austria
   d) Italy

3. Which country has a dragon on its flag?
   a) China
   b) Wales
   c) New Zealand
   d) Bhutan

4. Which Scandinavian country's flag is blue with a yellow cross?
   a) Denmark
   b) Finland
   c) Sweden
   d) Norway

5. Which country's flag is made up of black, green, and yellow horizontal stripes?
   a) Ghana
   b) South Africa
   c) Jamaica
   d) Tanzania

6. The Union Jack appears on the flag of which country?
   a) Canada
   b) New Zealand
   c) India
   d) France

7. Which country has an emblem of an eagle eating a snake on its flag?
   a) Spain
   b) Mexico
   c) Greece
   d) Egypt

8. The flag of which European country is red, white, and green?
   a) France
   b) Germany
   c) Italy
   d) Belgium

9. Which Asian country's flag is white with a red circle in the center?
   a) South Korea
   b) China
   c) Japan
   d) Thailand

10. Which country's flag features a blue and white star of David?
   a) Egypt
   b) Lebanon
   c) Israel
   d) Jordan

Intermediate:

1. Which African country's flag has a Kalashnikov rifle as part of its emblem?
   a) Chad
   b) Mozambique
   c) Kenya
   d) Nigeria

2. Which country's flag consists of two horizontal blue stripes with a white space in between?
   a) Greece
   b) Argentina
   c) Uruguay
   d) Honduras

3. Which South American country's flag features a sun with a face?
   a) Brazil
   b) Argentina
   c) Chile
   d) Peru

4. Which country's flag features an AK-47 crossed with a hoe?
   a) Angola
   b) Zimbabwe
   c) Uganda
   d) Sudan

5. Which country's flag consists of three vertical stripes in the order green, white, and red?
   a) Mexico
   b) Italy
   c) Ireland
   d) India

6. The Cedar tree is found on the flag of which country?
   a) Lebanon
   b) Syria
   c) Iraq
   d) Saudi Arabia

7. The flag of Nepal is unique because it is...
   a) Round
   b) Triangular
   c) Non-rectangular
   d) Double-sided

8. Which of these countries has the Southern Cross constellation on its flag?
   a) Canada
   b) New Zealand
   c) UK
   d) India

9. The flag of Belize features which of the following prominently in its center?
   a) A lion
   b) Two humans
   c) A bald eagle
   d) A maple leaf

10. Which island nation's flag features a trident?
   a) Jamaica
   b) Fiji
   c) Barbados
   d) Maldives

Challenging:

1. The "Lion of Judah" appears on the flag of which country?
   a) Israel
   b) Ethiopia
   c) Jordan
   d) Kenya

2. Which country's flag features a crane with one leg raised, carrying a stick?
   a) Uganda
   b) Tanzania
   c) Rwanda
   d) Zambia

3. Which country's flag contains 27 stars, representing its federal units?
   a) USA
   b) Australia
   c) Brazil
   d) Russia

4. The flag of which country consists of a white square in the center, containing a red cross, a red square in each corner, and a smaller white square inside each red square?
   a) Switzerland
   b) Denmark
   c) Georgia
   d) Finland

5. Which country's flag depicts a Simorgh (a mythological bird) and is often associated with its Zoroastrian heritage?
   a) India
   b) Iran
   c) Turkey
   d) Egypt

6. The flag of which country features a blue field with a yellow sun in the center and a yellow crescent moon and a star?
   a) Malaysia
   b) Kazakhstan
   c) Indonesia
   d) Pakistan

7. The flag of which country has a diagonal cross dividing it into four triangles, two green and two black?
   a) Ghana
   b) Kenya
   c) Jamaica
   d) Nigeria

8. Which flag features a chakra (wheel) in the center?
   a) Sri Lanka
   b) Nepal
   c) Bhutan
   d) India

9. Which country's flag, known as the "Five Provinces Flag," has a design representing its five major regions?
   a) China
   b) South Korea
   c) Japan
   d) Vietnam

10. The two blue stripes on the flag of Costa Rica represent...
   a) The Pacific and Caribbean oceans
   b) The two major rivers
   c) The two mountain ranges
   d) The past and the future

Expert:

1. The flag of Kyrgyzstan features a...
    a) Yurt's tunduk
    b) Mountain range
    c) Crescent moon
    d) Stylized eagle

2. Which of the following flags includes a representation of the biblical King Solomon's seal?
    a) Israel
    b) Ethiopia
    c) Morocco
    d) Jordan

3. The flag of the Isle of Man features what emblem?
    a) Three-legged triskele
    b) A lion rampant
    c) A double-headed eagle
    d) A dragon

4. Which country's flag was inspired by the French Tricolore but rotated 90 degrees?
    a) Italy
    b) Romania
    c) Belgium
    d) Netherlands

5. Which country's flag includes a depiction of Mount Ararat with Noah's Ark on top?
    a) Israel
    b) Jordan
    c) Armenia
    d) Turkey

6. The Pan-African colors, red, black, and green, were first adopted in the flag of which country?
   a) Ghana
   b) South Africa
   c) Kenya
   d) Libya

7. The flag of which country includes a koru, a Māori symbol representing a fern frond?
   a) New Zealand
   b) Fiji
   c) Australia
   d) Samoa

8. The flag of which Asian country includes a red field with a golden, 14-pointed star and crescent?
   a) Malaysia
   b) Indonesia
   c) Vietnam
   d) Brunei

9. The flag of which country includes a Vytis, a white knight on horseback holding a sword and shield?
   a) Estonia
   b) Latvia
   c) Belarus
   d) Lithuania

10. The flag of which country was the world's first to be designed using a specific, mathematical design process?
   a) Canada
   b) South Africa
   c) Fiji
   d) Mauritius

Urban Legends & Myths

Easy:

1. Which creature is said to inhabit Loch Ness in Scotland?
   a) Bigfoot
   b) Yeti
   c) Nessie
   d) Chupacabra

2. The legend of which headless horseman is popular in Sleepy Hollow, New York?
   a) The Dullahan
   b) The White Lady
   c) Kelpie
   d) The Headless Horseman

3. Which creature is often said to be found in the Himalayan mountains?
   a) Bigfoot
   b) Yeti
   c) Mothman
   d) Wendigo

4. Baba Yaga is a witch-like character from the folklore of which country?
   a) Ireland
   b) Japan
   c) Russia
   d) Brazil

5. Which legendary city is said to have sunk beneath the sea?
   a) El Dorado
   b) Atlantis
   c) Shangri-La
   d) Avalon

6. Which creature is associated with UFO sightings in West Virginia in the 1960s?
   a) Jersey Devil
   b) Mothman
   c) Spring-Heeled Jack
   d) Black Shuck

7. In which country is the vampire-like creature called "Chupacabra" commonly reported?
   a) Australia
   b) Mexico
   c) India
   d) Egypt

8. The legend of King Arthur is commonly associated with which mystical object?
   a) Magic Carpet
   b) Golden Fleece
   c) Excalibur
   d) Pandora's Box

9. Which creature from Japanese folklore is known for luring people into the water to drown?
   a) Kitsune
   b) Kelpie
   c) Kappa
   d) Tengu

10. The Fountain of Youth, a legendary spring that restores youth to anyone who drinks its waters, was sought after by which explorer?
   a) Christopher Columbus
   b) Hernán Cortés
   c) Ponce de León
   d) Marco Polo

Intermediate:

1. The "Highgate Vampire" is a legend from which city?
   a) Rome
   b) Paris
   c) London
   d) Berlin

2. Which legendary creature is said to lead travelers astray in deserts or forests?
   a) Will-o'-the-wisp
   b) Mermaid
   c) Phoenix
   d) Sphinx

3. In Norse mythology, who is the trickster god?
   a) Thor
   b) Odin
   c) Freyja
   d) Loki

4. The Minotaur, a creature with the head of a bull and body of a man, was imprisoned in a labyrinth on which island?
   a) Sicily
   b) Rhodes
   c) Crete
   d) Malta

5. Which of these is NOT a creature from Australian Aboriginal mythology?
   a) Tiddalik
   b) Bunyip
   c) Wendigo
   d) Rainbow Serpent

6. The legendary city of El Dorado was said to be full of what?
   a) Silver
   b) Spices
   c) Gold
   d) Diamonds

7. The kraken is a sea monster from the folklore of which country?
   a) Greece
   b) Japan
   c) Norway
   d) Canada

8. Which mythical creature is often depicted as a horse with a single, spiraled horn projecting from its forehead?
   a) Griffin
   b) Unicorn
   c) Chimera
   d) Harpy

9. La Llorona, a ghostly woman who mourns her drowned children, is a legend from which culture?
   a) Chinese
   b) Mexican
   c) Russian
   d) Egyptian

10. Which mythical creature from Irish folklore is known to foretell death by wailing?
    a) Banshee
    b) Goblin
    c) Gorgon
    d) Djinn

Challenging:

1. Which legendary African city was said to be made entirely of gold?
    a) Zerzura
    b) Timbuktu
    c) Ophir
    d) The Lost City of the Kalahari

2. The "Jersey Devil" is associated with which U.S. state?
    a) New York
    b) Delaware
    c) New Jersey
    d) Maryland

3. Which of these creatures is said to live in the Pine Barrens of New Jersey?
    a) Mothman
    b) Wendigo
    c) Jersey Devil
    d) Chupacabra

4. The Crying Boy is a mass-produced print of a painting that is allegedly cursed. What is said to happen to homes that have this painting?
    a) They get robbed
    b) They experience good luck
    c) They get infested with pests
    d) They catch fire

5. Which mythical creature was said to reside in the forests of North America and has its roots in Algonquian myths?
    a) Chupacabra
    b) Wendigo
    c) Nephilim
    d) Selkie

6. "Drop bears" are a fictional Australian creature used to playfully scare tourists. They are said to be a predatory version of which real animal?
   a) Koala
   b) Kangaroo
   c) Wombat
   d) Platypus

7. The Catacombs beneath which city are said to be haunted?
   a) Venice
   b) London
   c) Paris
   d) Rome

8. The Lady in White or White Lady legends often involve a ghostly figure dressed in white. What is the common theme of these legends?
   a) Revenge
   b) Lost love or sorrow
   c) Greed
   d) Betrayal

9. Which creature from Slavic folklore is known for its malicious nature and its ability to impersonate loved ones?
   a) Doppelgänger
   b) Poltergeist
   c) Baba Yaga
   d) Domovoi

10. According to legend, the city of Troy was taken by the Greeks using what?
   a) A massive battering ram
   b) A hidden tunnel
   c) A giant crossbow
   d) A wooden horse

Expert:

1. In the Arthurian legend, which lake did the Lady of the Lake reside in?
   a) Lake Geneva
   b) Loch Ness
   c) Lake Nemi
   d) Dozmary Pool

2. The legend of the "Flying Dutchman" concerns a ghostly what?
   a) Airplane
   b) Train
   c) Ship
   d) Carriage

3. The "Mothman" sightings in the 1960s were associated with the collapse of which structure?
   a) Tacoma Narrows Bridge
   b) Silver Bridge
   c) Sunshine Skyway Bridge
   d) Tappan Zee Bridge

4. Which legendary creature is said to inhabit the swamps of South Carolina and Georgia and is known for its eerie, haunting whistle?
   a) Jersey Devil
   b) Goatman
   c) Lizard Man
   d) Hodag

5. The "Bermuda Triangle" is notorious for what?
   a) Volcanic eruptions
   b) Disappearances of ships and planes
   c) Pirate attacks
   d) Giant whirlpools

6. According to Aztec legend, the city of Tenochtitlan (modern-day Mexico City) was founded on the spot where an eagle was seen doing what?
  a) Carrying a snake
  b) Perched on a cactus
  c) Fighting with a jaguar
  d) Both a) and b)

7. Which legendary figure is said to reside in the Green Mountains of Vermont and to protect its animals and environment?
  a) Bigfoot
  b) Mothman
  c) Chupacabra
  d) The Green Mountain Phantom

8. The Golem is a creature from Jewish folklore. What is it made of?
  a) Stone
  b) Wood
  c) Clay
  d) Water

9. Which island is associated with the legend of the "Blue Men of the Minch", who challenge passersby to a rhyming contest?
  a) Isle of Man
  b) Isle of Skye
  c) Isle of Wight
  d) Isle of Mull

10. The Wendigo legend speaks of a creature that is insatiably hungry for what?
  a) Gold
  b) Human flesh
  c) Water
  d) Fire

Flora and Fauna

Easy:

1. Which animal is known as the "King of the Jungle"?
   a) Lion
   b) Elephant
   c) Tiger
   d) Cheetah

2. Which tree is known for its bright red leaves in autumn?
   a) Oak
   b) Birch
   c) Maple
   d) Pine

3. What is the largest mammal in the world?
   a) Elephant
   b) Whale Shark
   c) Blue Whale
   d) Giraffe

4. Which of these is a marsupial?
   a) Raccoon
   b) Kangaroo
   c) Bear
   d) Tiger

5. What type of creature is a python?
   a) Bird
   b) Mammal
   c) Reptile
   d) Amphibian

6. Which plant is known for its spines and is adapted to desert conditions?
   a) Cactus
   b) Oak
   c) Fern
   d) Moss

7. Which bird is known for its beautiful tail feathers and mating dance?
   a) Ostrich
   b) Peacock
   c) Sparrow
   d) Eagle

8. Which animal is the tallest in the world?
   a) Elephant
   b) Blue Whale
   c) Ostrich
   d) Giraffe

9. Which flower is associated with Holland?
   a) Rose
   b) Tulip
   c) Lily
   d) Sunflower

10. What kind of animal is a grizzly?
   a) Fish
   b) Bird
   c) Bear
   d) Reptile

Intermediate:

1. Which continent is the native home of the kangaroo?
   a) Africa
   b) South America
   c) Australia
   d) North America

2. Which tree produces acorns?
   a) Pine
   b) Maple
   c) Oak
   d) Birch

3. The poison dart frog is native to which region?
   a) Deserts of Africa
   b) Amazon Rainforest
   c) Siberian tundras
   d) European grasslands

4. Which of these flowers is known to trap insects?
   a) Rose
   b) Sunflower
   c) Venus Flytrap
   d) Tulip

5. Which of the following is a flightless bird?
   a) Peacock
   b) Kiwi
   c) Sparrow
   d) Falcon

6. Which marine creature has tentacles and is known for its sting?
   a) Shark
   b) Dolphin
   c) Starfish
   d) Jellyfish

7. What is the primary diet of a panda bear?
   a) Meat
   b) Honey
   c) Bamboo
   d) Berries

8. Which of these animals is known to migrate in large groups across the Serengeti?
   a) Elephant
   b) Wildebeest
   c) Tiger
   d) Kangaroo

9. Which tree is traditionally used as a Christmas tree?
   a) Oak
   b) Spruce
   c) Maple
   d) Birch

10. Which animal is known as the "ship of the desert"?
   a) Camel
   b) Elephant
   c) Horse
   d) Llama

Challenging:

1. What is the world's smallest flowering plant?
   a) Redwood
   b) Duckweed
   c) Sunflower
   d) Rose

2. Which animal can be found at the top of the marine food chain?
   a) Jellyfish
   b) Krill
   c) Orca
   d) Clownfish

3. Which plant is known to live for thousands of years?
   a) Grass
   b) Rose
   c) Bristlecone Pine
   d) Fern

4. Which bird has the largest wingspan in the world?
   a) Falcon
   b) Peacock
   c) Albatross
   d) Sparrow

5. Which of these is not a type of marsupial?
   a) Koala
   b) Wallaby
   c) Raccoon
   d) Wombat

6. What type of animal is the peregrine falcon?
   a) Rodent
   b) Fish
   c) Bird of prey
   d) Mammal

7. Which tree sheds its bark instead of its leaves?
   a) Eucalyptus
   b) Oak
   c) Birch
   d) Maple

8. The rafflesia plant is known for what distinctive feature?
   a) Vibrant colors
   b) Producing the world's largest flower
   c) Glowing in the dark
   d) Producing music

9. Which of these animals is a marsupial native to North America?
   a) Kangaroo
   b) Opossum
   c) Koala
   d) Tasmanian Devil

10. Which bird is known as the "bird of paradise" due to its stunning appearance?
   a) Sparrow
   b) Kiwi
   c) Phoenix
   d) Cendrawasih

Expert:

1. What is the name of the world's rarest and most endangered tree?
   a) Wollemi Pine
   b) Red Maple
   c) Blue Spruce
   d) Silver Birch

2. Which animal has a heart that can weigh up to 15 pounds?
   a) Elephant
   b) Blue Whale
   c) Giraffe
   d) Orca

3. Which plant has the ability to reproduce both sexually and asexually?
   a) Fern
   b) Oak tree
   c) Dandelion
   d) Rose

4. The axolotl, a type of salamander that never undergoes metamorphosis, is native to which country?
   a) Brazil
   b) Japan
   c) Mexico
   d) Canada

5. What is the name of the fungus that has a mutualistic relationship with tree roots, enhancing nutrient uptake?
   a) Lichen
   b) Moss
   c) Mycorrhizae
   d) Mold

6. Which bird can mimic almost any sound it hears, including chainsaws?
   a) Raven
   b) Lyrebird
   c) Parrot
   d) Nightingale

7. The corpse flower has a unique smell resembling what?
   a) Fresh roses
   b) Rotten flesh
   c) Freshly baked bread
   d) Lemon zest

8. Which mammal has the ability to fly?
   a) Squirrel
   b) Bat
   c) Puma
   d) Dolphin

9. The Sundew plant captures its prey with what?
   a) Sharp thorns
   b) Underground traps
   c) Sticky tentacles
   d) Loud sounds

10. Which sea creature can regenerate lost limbs?
   a) Dolphin
   b) Shark
   c) Starfish
   d) Jellyfish

World Cuisine

Easy:

1. Which country is famous for sushi?
   a) Italy
   b) India
   c) Russia
   d) Japan

2. Which dish is a popular Spanish tapa made of tomatoes, cucumbers, and onions?
   a) Gazpacho
   b) Tandoori
   c) Paella
   d) Guacamole

3. Which country is known for its pasta dishes?
   a) China
   b) Italy
   c) Mexico
   d) Greece

4. From which country does the dessert "baklava" originate?
   a) Italy
   b) Turkey
   c) India
   d) Brazil

5. Which country introduced "tacos" to world cuisine?
   a) Spain
   b) Mexico
   c) Italy
   d) India

6. Which of these dishes is a type of Indian bread?
   a) Fajita
   b) Tempura
   c) Naan
   d) Risotto

7. Croissant is associated with the bakery of which country?
   a) France
   b) Germany
   c) Sweden
   d) Canada

8. Which country is famous for making chocolate?
   a) Switzerland
   b) Russia
   c) Mexico
   d) Australia

9. Which dish is made from thinly sliced raw fish?
   a) Tempura
   b) Sashimi
   c) Falafel
   d) Churros

10. Dim sum is a popular dish in which Asian country?
   a) Vietnam
   b) Japan
   c) China
   d) Thailand

Intermediate:

1. Feijoada is a traditional dish of which country?
   a) Argentina
   b) Brazil
   c) Chile
   d) Peru

2. Which country's cuisine includes "kimchi" as a staple?
   a) China
   b) Japan
   c) South Korea
   d) Thailand

3. In which country would you find the dish "moussaka"?
   a) Greece
   b) Italy
   c) Turkey
   d) Spain

4. Which of the following dishes is a traditional Filipino delicacy made from a duck embryo?
   a) Dim sum
   b) Satay
   c) Balut
   d) Adobo

5. Haggis is a traditional dish of which country?
   a) Scotland
   b) Ireland
   c) Wales
   d) England

6. Which of these is a spicy soup commonly consumed in Thailand?
   a) Udon
   b) Pho
   c) Tom Yum
   d) Borscht

7. Which Middle Eastern dish is primarily made of chickpeas?
   a) Shawarma
   b) Falafel
   c) Gyro
   d) Kofta

8. Which country is known for its wine regions, including Bordeaux and Champagne?
   a) Spain
   b) Italy
   c) France
   d) Portugal

9. "Poutine" is a popular dish in which country?
   a) Australia
   b) Canada
   c) United States
   d) New Zealand

10. From which country does the spicy condiment "harissa" originate?
   a) India
   b) Turkey
   c) Tunisia
   d) Mexico

Challenging:

1. The dish "ceviche" primarily consists of what?
   a) Raw fish
   b) Cooked beef
   c) Boiled vegetables
   d) Fried chicken

2. Rendang, a slow-cooked dry curry deeply spiced with ginger and turmeric, is a delicacy in which country?
   a) India
   b) Indonesia
   c) Thailand
   d) Vietnam

3. "Lutefisk" is a traditional dish of which country, known for its unique preparation involving lye?
   a) Denmark
   b) Sweden
   c) Germany
   d) Poland

4. Which country is known for its "borscht" soup?
   a) Germany
   b) Poland
   c) Russia
   d) Hungary

5. The dish "kare-kare" is a type of stew made with peanut sauce and is a delicacy in which country?
   a) Thailand
   b) Vietnam
   c) Malaysia
   d) Philippines

6. "Sauerbraten" is a pot roast, usually of beef, marinated in a mixture including vinegar or wine, from which country?
   a) Austria
   b) Switzerland
   c) Germany
   d) Belgium

7. Which dish, meaning "under the bell", involves slow cooking meat and vegetables under a dome-shaped ceramic lid?
   a) Peka
   b) Tagine
   c) Biryani
   d) Ratatouille

8. Which country is famous for "smørrebrød", an open-faced sandwich on rye bread?
   a) Norway
   b) Denmark
   c) Finland
   d) Iceland

9. "Fufu" is a staple dish in many African countries, made from what?
   a) Ground beef
   b) Rice
   c) Mashed starchy vegetables
   d) Lentils

10. "Pierogi" are filled dumplings that are a traditional dish in which country?
   a) Italy
   b) Poland
   c) Russia
   d) Greece

Expert:

1. Which fermented food is a staple in Bhutanese cuisine?
   a) Kimchi
   b) Sauerkraut
   c) Ema datshi
   d) Tempeh

2. "Surströmming" is a type of fermented fish considered a delicacy in which country?
   a) Finland
   b) Norway
   c) Sweden
   d) Denmark

3. Which country has a traditional dish called "Acarajé", made from black-eyed peas formed into a ball and then deep-fried?
   a) Argentina
   b) Mexico
   c) Brazil
   d) Peru

4. "Teurgoule" is a rice pudding from which region?
   a) Catalonia, Spain
   b) Normandy, France
   c) Tuscany, Italy
   d) Bavaria, Germany

5. Which country has a dish called "Hákarl", which is made from fermented shark?
   a) Iceland
   b) Norway
   c) Greenland
   d) Finland

6. "Bebinca" is a traditional dessert from which state in India?
   a) Kerala
   b) Goa
   c) Maharashtra
   d) Tamil Nadu

7. "Century eggs" or "preserved eggs", often consumed in China, are made by preserving duck, chicken or quail eggs in a mixture of clay, ash, and salt for several weeks to months. How do they appear when cut open?
   a) Bright yellow
   b) Reddish-brown
   c) Greenish-black
   d) White

8. "Amok trey" is a Cambodian dish made with fish steamed in coconut milk and spices. How is it typically served?
   a) In a bamboo shoot
   b) Wrapped in banana leaves
   c) On a bed of rice noodles
   d) In a hollowed-out pineapple

9. Which country's national dish is "Saltah", a stew that contains fenugreek froth and is usually served with flatbread?
   a) Oman
   b) Yemen
   c) Lebanon
   d) Jordan

10. Which dish from Georgia is a type of bread filled with melted cheese, and sometimes egg and butter?
   a) Goulash
   b) Khachapuri
   c) Moussaka
   d) Kolach

Answers

Easy:

1. b) New York City
2. d) Paris
3. b) Venice
4. a) Beijing
5. b) Paris
6. a) Rio de Janeiro
7. b) Rome
8. a) Mumbai
9. c) France
10. b) Moscow

Intermediate:

1. b) Istanbul
2. c) Wellington
3. b) Amsterdam
4. c) Dubai
5. b) Jordan
6. c) Siem Reap
7. b) Rio de Janeiro
8. a) Mali
9. b) Venice
10. b) Pamplona

Challenging:

1. b) Stockholm
2. b) Goa
3. d) Damascus
4. c) Brussels
5. a) Istanbul
6. c) Peru
7. d) Port
8. c) Istanbul
9. c) Johannesburg
10. b) London

Expert:

1. c) Cairo
2. a) York
3. c) Lalibela
4. c) Tajikistan
5. c) Koror
6. c) Tunis
7. a) Mongolia
8. c) Shiraz
9. d) Ho Chi Minh City
10. b) Mosul

Famous Landmarks

Easy:

1. c) France
2. a) China
3. b) Italy
4. a) France
5. c) Rio de Janeiro
6. a) India
7. c) England
8. d) Sydney
9. c) Egypt
10. b) Pisa

Intermediate:

1. c) South Dakota
2. b) Jordan
3. b) Athens
4. c) Dubai
5. c) Chile
6. d) Siem Reap
7. b) Berlin
8. c) Germany
9. d) San Francisco
10. b) Beijing

Challenging:

1. a) Brussels
2. d) Florence
3. c) Peru
4. c) The Royal Crown Jewels
5. b) Barcelona
6. c) Morocco
7. c) France
8. c) Italy
9. c) New York City
10. c) Northern Ireland

Expert:

1. c) Norway
2. b) Greece
3. c) Turkmenistan
4. a) India
5. b) Timbuktu
6. c) Peru
7. c) China
8. a) Malta
9. a) Syria
10. b) Turkey

Easy:

1. c) England
2. c) Hinduism
3. c) Greece
4. a) Mexico
5. d) Haka
6. c) Japan
7. b) Brazil
8. a) Fireworks
9. b) Spain
10. c) Scotland

Intermediate:

1. d) Holi
2. b) China
3. a) Sweden
4. b) India
5. b) Russia
6. a) Bali
7. a) Kenya
8. c) Spain
9. b) Japan
10. c) Turkey

Challenging:

1. d) Japan
2. a) San Fermin
3. b) Hawaii
4. b) Indonesia
5. c) Peru
6. c) Northern Africa
7. a) Mongolia
8. b) China
9. b) Japan
10. c) Lebanon

Expert:

1. b) Madagascar
2. a) Central Africa
3. d) Sweden
4. a) Lapland
5. b) Trinidad and Tobago
6. c) Uzbekistan
7. a) Nepal
8. a) Ireland
9. c) Catalonia
10. a) Bear

Natural Wonders

Easy:

1. a) Mount Everest
2. b) USA and Canada
3. a) Brazil
4. c) Africa
5. b) Australia
6. c) Arizona
7. c) Tanzania
8. b) Israel
9. a) Bolivia
10. b) Zimbabwe

Intermediate:

1. d) Arctic Circle
2. a) Philippines
3. a) Ecuador
4. a) Yellowstone National Park
5. b) Vietnam
6. b) Lake Baikal
7. d) Northern Ireland
8. c) Venezuela
9. a) Chile
10. a) Bryce Canyon National Park

Challenging:

1. b) Seychelles
2. d) Turkmenistan
3. b) Plitvice Lakes National Park
4. c) Australia
5. b) Vietnam
6. c) Chile
7. b) Guyana
8. a) Iceland
9. a) Botswana
10. a) Canada

Expert:

1. a) Mid-Atlantic Ridge
2. c) Mauritania
3. d) Iceland
4. c) Venezuela
5. d) Antarctica
6. c) Ethiopia
7. c) Dominica
8. a) Yemen
9. b) Turkey
10. a) Madagascar

Oceans & Seas

Easy:

1. d) Pacific Ocean
2. a) Dead Sea
3. c) Arctic Ocean
4. a) Atlantic Ocean
5. b) Caspian Sea
6. d) Southern Ocean
7. a) Atlantic Ocean
8. a) Caribbean
9. a) Coral Sea
10. c) Mediterranean Sea

Intermediate:

1. b) Pacific Ocean
2. c) Caspian Sea
3. c) Ocean currents
4. c) Indian Ocean
5. c) Adriatic Sea
6. b) Russia
7. c) Indian Ocean
8. c) Indian Ocean
9. c) Atlantic Ocean
10. b) Papua New Guinea

Challenging:

1. d) Arctic Ocean
2. c) Arctic Ocean
3. b) Thailand
4. a) Strait of Gibraltar
5. c) South America and Antarctica
6. a) India
7. c) Persian Gulf
8. b) Norway
9. b) Sargasso Sea
10. d) Southern Ocean

Expert:

1. b) Adriatic Sea
2. a) Caspian Sea
3. d) India
4. b) Atlantic Ocean
5. b) Denmark Strait
6. c) Tasman Sea
7. c) Antarctica
8. b) Gulf of Mexico
9. a) USA and Canada
10. b) Convergent boundary

Easy:

1. c) Temperature
2. c) Dew
3. d) Carbon dioxide
4. a) Desert
5. c) A rotating column of air
6. a) Troposphere
7. b) Front
8. c) Nebulus
9. b) Rain or stormy weather
10. d) Fujita scale

Intermediate:

1. d) Warm and dry summers
2. b) El Niño
3. b) Weather is short-term, climate is long-term.
4. d) South Asia
5. d) Atacama Desert
6. d) Nitrogen
7. d) Cumulonimbus
8. c) Pacific
9. d) Marseille, France
10. b) An intense dust storm

Challenging:

1. a) El Niño
2. a) Mawsynram, India (Although, Cherrapunji, which is nearby, also claims this title occasionally, so both could be correct based on recent data)
3. c) Jet stream
4. c) Subarctic
5. b) Mesosphere
6. a) Wind shear
7. a) El Niño
8. b) Gobi Desert
9. b) Atmospheric pressure
10. b) Himalayas

Expert:

1. a) Rain that evaporates before reaching the ground
2. c) Heavy precipitation and thunderstorms
3. c) Alpine
4. b) Differences in salinity and temperature
5. b) Stratosphere
6. c) The Alps in Europe
7. c) DANA (Depresión Aislada en Niveles Altos)
8. a) Sahara Air Layer
9. c) Increase in city temperatures, especially at night
10. b) A brief, intense downburst of wind from a thunderstorm

Easy:

1. c) Nile
2. b) Caspian Sea
3. c) London
4. c) Hinduism
5. b) Lake Baikal
6. b) Mediterranean Sea
7. b) USA
8. d) Volga
9. b) Bolivia
10. c) Lake Titicaca

Intermediate:

1. a) Colorado River
2. d) 14
3. c) Lake Como
4. c) Mesopotamians
5. c) Ural
6. b) Peru
7. d) Uganda
8. c) Brahmaputra
9. b) France
10. c) Saint Lawrence River

Challenging:

1. d) Rio Grande
2. d) Philippines
3. d) Both b) and c)
4. b) Yellow River (Huang He)
5. c) Contains more water than the North American Great Lakes combined
6. d) Zambezi River
7. a) Amazon
8. d) Lake Tahoe
9. c) Himalayas
10. c) Nile

Expert:

1. c) Both a) and b)
2. c) Antarctica
3. a) Congo
4. d) A delta
5. c) Its size varies dramatically between wet and dry seasons.
6. b) Río de la Plata
7. b) India
8. b) Lena
9. c) Its nightly lightning phenomena.
10. c) Myanmar and Thailand

Easy:

1. a) Hanging Gardens
2. b) Rio de Janeiro
3. c) Paris
4. c) Colossus of Rhodes
5. b) Nomadic Tribes
6. c) Colosseum
7. c) Agra
8. a) Mausoleum at Halicarnassus
9. c) Australia
10. b) Statue of Zeus

Intermediate:

1. a) Temple of Artemis
2. d) Dubai
3. b) Suez Canal
4. b) France
5. d) South Dakota
6. c) France
7. b) Machu Picchu
8. c) Germany
9. d) San Francisco
10. a) Venice

Challenging:

1. c) Stonehenge
2. b) Jordan
3. b) Istanbul
4. c) Great Wall of China
5. b) Machu Picchu
6. c) Bell Tower
7. d) Taj Mahal
8. d) Malbork Castle
9. b) Granada, Spain
10. c) Japan

Expert:

1. d) The Prague Orloj
2. d) Indonesia
3. b) Sagrada Família
4. d) Quebec City
5. c) Tiahuanaco
6. a) The Kremlin, Moscow
7. c) Great Wall of China
8. a) The Gur-e Amir
9. c) Istanbul
10. c) Easter Island Statues

Easy:

1. c) Easter Island
2. d) Indonesia
3. c) Ireland
4. c) New York City
5. a) Jamaica
6. c) New Zealand
7. c) Italy
8. d) Greenland
9. b) Jamaica
10. a) Galápagos Islands

Intermediate:

1. b) Indian
2. d) Iceland
3. c) Corsica
4. a) Sri Lanka
5. c) Bay of Bengal
6. c) Crete
7. a) Sicily
8. b) Indonesia
9. a) Between England and Ireland
10. b) Society Islands

Challenging:

1. b) Fraser Island
2. b) Indonesia
3. a) Bali
4. d) Komodo
5. c) Newfoundland
6. b) Indian
7. a) Pitcairn Island
8. d) Balearic Islands
9. c) Sri Lanka
10. b) Crete

Expert:

1. a) Taiwan
2. b) Easter Island
3. a) Borneo
4. a) Krakatoa
5. b) Hawaii
6. b) Hawaii
7. d) Madagascar
8. a) Arctic Ocean
9. c) Tasmania
10. d) None of the above (it's in Costa Rica, which is not an island)

Easy:

1. c) Canada
2. c) Austria
3. b) Wales
4. c) Sweden
5. d) Tanzania
6. b) New Zealand
7. b) Mexico
8. c) Italy
9. c) Japan
10. c) Israel

Intermediate:

1. b) Mozambique
2. a) Greece
3. b) Argentina
4. a) Angola
5. a) Mexico
6. a) Lebanon
7. c) Non-rectangular
8. b) New Zealand
9. b) Two humans
10. c) Barbados

Challenging:

1. b) Ethiopia
2. a) Uganda
3. c) Brazil
4. c) Georgia
5. b) Iran
6. a) Malaysia
7. c) Jamaica
8. d) India
9. b) South Korea
10. a) The Pacific and Caribbean oceans

Expert:

1. a) Yurt's tunduk
2. b) Ethiopia
3. a) Three-legged triskele
4. a) Italy
5. c) Armenia
6. a) Ghana
7. a) New Zealand
8. d) Brunei
9. d) Lithuania
10. d) Mauritius

Easy:

1. c) Nessie
2. d) The Headless Horseman
3. b) Yeti
4. c) Russia
5. b) Atlantis
6. b) Mothman
7. b) Mexico
8. c) Excalibur
9. c) Kappa
10. c) Ponce de León

Intermediate:

1. c) London
2. a) Will-o'-the-wisp
3. d) Loki
4. c) Crete
5. c) Wendigo
6. c) Gold
7. c) Norway
8. b) Unicorn
9. b) Mexican
10. a) Banshee

Challenging:

1. b) Timbuktu
2. c) New Jersey
3. c) Jersey Devil
4. d) They catch fire
5. b) Wendigo
6. a) Koala
7. c) Paris
8. b) Lost love or sorrow
9. d) Domovoi
10. d) A wooden horse

Expert:

1. d) Dozmary Pool
2. c) Ship
3. b) Silver Bridge
4. c) Lizard Man
5. b) Disappearances of ships and planes
6. d) Both a) and b)
7. d) The Green Mountain Phantom
8. c) Clay
9. b) Isle of Skye
10. b) Human flesh

Easy:

1. a) Lion
2. c) Maple
3. c) Blue Whale
4. b) Kangaroo
5. c) Reptile
6. a) Cactus
7. b) Peacock
8. d) Giraffe
9. b) Tulip
10. c) Bear

Intermediate:

1. c) Australia
2. c) Oak
3. b) Amazon Rainforest
4. c) Venus Flytrap
5. b) Kiwi
6. d) Jellyfish
7. c) Bamboo
8. b) Wildebeest
9. b) Spruce
10. a) Camel

Challenging:

1. b) Duckweed
2. c) Orca
3. c) Bristlecone Pine
4. c) Albatross
5. c) Raccoon
6. c) Bird of prey
7. a) Eucalyptus
8. b) Producing the world's largest flower
9. b) Opossum
10. d) Cendrawasih

Expert:

1. a) Wollemi Pine
2. b) Blue Whale
3. c) Dandelion
4. c) Mexico
5. c) Mycorrhizae
6. b) Lyrebird
7. b) Rotten flesh
8. b) Bat
9. c) Sticky tentacles
10. c) Starfish

Easy:

1. d) Japan
2. a) Gazpacho
3. b) Italy
4. b) Turkey
5. b) Mexico
6. c) Naan
7. a) France
8. a) Switzerland
9. b) Sashimi
10. c) China

Intermediate:

1. b) Brazil
2. c) South Korea
3. a) Greece
4. c) Balut
5. a) Scotland
6. c) Tom Yum
7. b) Falafel
8. c) France
9. b) Canada
10. c) Tunisia

Challenging:

1. a) Raw fish
2. b) Indonesia
3. b) Sweden
4. c) Russia
5. d) Philippines
6. c) Germany
7. a) Peka
8. b) Denmark
9. c) Mashed starchy vegetables
10. b) Poland

Expert:

1. c) Ema datshi
2. c) Sweden
3. c) Brazil
4. b) Normandy, France
5. a) Iceland
6. b) Goa
7. c) Greenish-black
8. b) Wrapped in banana leaves
9. b) Yemen
10. b) Khachapuri

Made in the USA
Las Vegas, NV
18 December 2024

14602330R00075